ASSISTED SUICIDE

Mark Friedman

www.raintreepublishers.co.uk
Visit our website to find out
more information about
Raintree books.

To order:
☎ Phone 0845 6044371
🖨 Fax +44 (0) 1865 312263
📧 Email myorders@raintreepublishers.co.uk

Customers from outside the UK please telephone +44 1865 312262

Raintree is an imprint of Capstone Global Library
Limited, a company incorporated in England and
Wales having its registered office at 7 Pilgrim
Street, London, EC4V 6LB – Registered company
number: 6695582

Edited by Adam Miller, Andrew Farrow, and Adrian
    Vigliano
Designed by Clare Webber and Steve Mead
Original illustrations © Capstone Global Library
    Ltd
Picture research by Ruth Blair
Production by Eirian Griffiths
Originated by Capstone Global Library Ltd
Printed and bound in China by Leo Paper Group
    Ltd

ISBN 978 1 406 22373 6
15 14 13 12
10 9 8 7 6 5 4 3 2

British Library Cataloguing in Publication Data

Friedman, Mark D.
Assisted suicide. – (Hot topics)
179.7-dc22
A full catalogue record for this book is available
from the British Library.

Acknowledgements

We would like to thank the following for
permission to reproduce photographs: Alamy
pp. **16** (PhotoStockFile), **18** (KAKIMAGE), **21**
(© Image Source), **35** (Photofusion Picture
Library), **39** (Travelscape Images), **45** (© Neil
Tingle); Corbis pp. **10** (© Julie Fisher), **12** (©
Rubberball), **15** (© Handout Courtesy of the
Schiavo Family), **25** (© Rob Kim/Retna Ltd), **26**
(© ER Productions), **29** (© Dean Lewins/epa), **30**
(© Image Source); Getty Images pp. **5**, **7** (Simon
Roberts), **24**, **33** (SSPL), **42** (Susan M. Gaetz),
49 (BEN STANSALL/AFP); PA Photos pp. **4** (Jane
Tomlinson/Bindmans), **23** (AP Photo/Richard
Sheinwald), **41** (PA Archive), **47** (EMPICS Sport),
51 (Parents of Andrew Devine).

Cover photograph of a woman's hand in the palm
of a man's hand reproduced with permission
of Getty Images (Ruth Jenkinson/Dorling
Kindersley).

Disclaimer

CONTENTS

Some words are printed in bold, **like this**. You can find out what they mean by looking in the glossary.

CONTROLLING THE END OF LIFE

Tony Nicklinson, a healthy middle-aged Englishman, suffers a **stroke**. He is **paralyzed** from the neck down. He loses the ability to speak. He can only communicate by nodding his head, and he cannot feed, bathe, or dress himself. After five years of living in this "locked-in syndrome", his doctors believe he will never improve significantly. This will be his condition for the rest of his life.

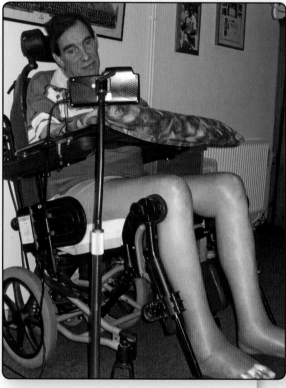

■ Tony Nicklinson says he wishes doctors had not saved his life.

Vincent Humbert is a 22-year-old Frenchman who is injured severely in a car accident. He loses his vision and his ability to speak, and he is paralyzed from the neck down. His mother turns her life upside down to care for him, but he only wants to die to end the suffering for them both. Only able to use his right thumb to point to letters of the alphabet, he writes a letter to French President Jacques Chirac, pleading for the right to end his life. Chirac denies the request. Vincent then writes an entire book, I Ask For The Right To Die, to make his case public.

■ Vincent Humbert's mother Marie, at a press conference, three years after helping her son to die.

Fighting for the right to die

Countless people have their lives interrupted by tragedies similar to those faced by Tony Nicklinson and Vincent Humbert. Most of these stories never make the headlines. But these two men became famous from the legal battles they or their families fought. Tony Nicklinson and his family have fought the British government in court for his right to die. Vincent Humbert fought the French government. He eventually died when his mother gave him a deadly dose of medication. (She was arrested briefly and then released.)

The choice to end life

To commit **suicide** is to intentionally kill oneself for one of many reasons: depression, mental illness, drug or alcohol addiction, or some tragedy in a person's life. Typically, people will commit suicide because they are not able to see possible solutions to their problems or a fulfilling, happy future.

But people who have life-ending illnesses or other serious medical conditions may not have a future or any choices. Sometimes they seek ways to end their lives as peacefully and painlessly as possible. Some seek **euthanasia**, also called "mercy killing", in which a doctor agrees with a patient or the patient's family to cause the end of the patient's life. Others seek **assisted suicide**, in which a doctor, family member, or friend help the patient end his or her life.

We can all sympathize with any person whose life reaches such a tragic point. But not everyone agrees that individuals should be able to cause their own deaths, even in extreme cases of suffering. Around the world, different cultures have different beliefs, and different countries have different laws concerning euthanasia and assisted suicide. No matter where you live, the topic is loaded with intense emotion and controversy.

WHY PEOPLE CHOOSE DEATH

Human beings are the only animals on Earth that can truly control most of what happens in their lives. We have minds, and we make decisions for ourselves. We decide where to live, our hobbies, and who we want to be friends with. We also make deep, personal decisions, such as our religious or political beliefs. And we make minor, everyday decisions, such as what to have for breakfast or whether to wear a jacket or not if it is chilly.

No matter how important the decision is, our freedom to decide represents our ability to control our own lives. Our freedom to decide is a unique human feature. It is part of the **dignity** of being a person.

Losing the power to choose

Have you ever been frustrated because you could not make important decisions for yourself? Everyone has known that frustration at one time or another. You feel like you lack control. Serious illness robs individuals of control and dignity. When you are ill, one decision after another is removed from your hands. The more serious the illness, the more control you lose.

If you have ever been hospitalised, you know what it is like. Privacy vanishes. You cannot wear your own clothes or sleep in your own bed. Doctors and nurses walk into your room at any hour of the day or night. Depending on the seriousness of your condition, you lose the ability to dress yourself, go to the bathroom by yourself, or bathe yourself. Luckily, most stays in a hospital do not last very long. You recover, go home, and return to normal life.

A difficult choice

But consider people with **terminal** illnesses. They will not recover and may never get to go home. They may already be enduring the pain from the illness itself and the unpleasant effects of surgery or treatment. On top of that, they lose all control, all privacy, and all freedom to live a normal life.

So, a choice appears in the minds of many people living under these circumstances. They may choose to die quickly and painlessly, rather than endure a life that does not really seem like a complete human life.

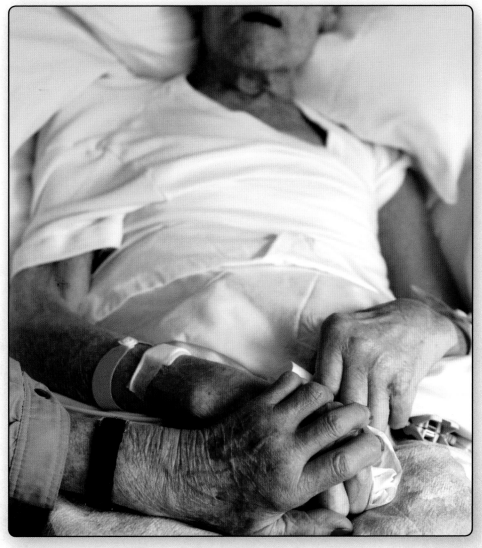

■ Terminally ill patients frequently decide that suicide is a better option than living through a very slow, painful death.

The difficulty of surviving

Today, doctors are able to cure many serious diseases. Scientific advances are always allowing doctors to provide new cures and treatments for a range of diseases.

On the one hand, we are truly lucky to live in an age of advanced science and medicine. But perhaps there is an unfortunate side to the wonders of medicine. Although there are treatments that extend our lives, these treatments can be painful and costly. Some people discover they cannot bear the treatment.

CASE STUDY

Hannah Jones

Hannah Jones, a British teenager, suffered from a hole in her heart. Her only chance of survival was heart transplant surgery. But after years of medical treatment, Hannah decided she could not endure any more surgery or hospitalization. She decided to die peacefully at home. Her parents supported her decision.

But government officials intervened and attempted to force Hannah to have the surgery. After a long struggle, Hannah changed her mind and decided to have the surgery. She endured a difficult recovery, but she did recover and went back to a normal life.

Think about this story. Do you think a person should be able to choose to refuse life-saving surgery? Do you think a government should be able to force someone to have surgery to save his or her life?

A life worth living?

Even more difficult is the situation of terminal illness. When people are **diagnosed** with diseases that are certain to kill them, they may be faced with long and difficult treatment – but to what end? Although the treatment may reduce some of the pain of the disease, the result of the treatment will still be death, not a cure.

Some people still feel relatively healthy when they are diagnosed with a terminal disease. They can still be active and productive in the last months of their lives. But if they start treatment, they could wind up hospitalised and be robbed of this happiness in their final days of life.

And what about people whose quality of life is greatly diminished due to accidents or injuries? These people sometimes feel that their quality of life is not worth living for.

These are among the many situations that can lead a person or a family to consider euthanasia or assisted suicide. The chart on the next page lists the most common reasons.

Common reasons people consider euthanasia and assisted suicide

Terminal disease	Chronic/progressive/ degenerative condition	Accident or injury
Terminal diseases will end a person's life, despite treatment. These diseases are treatable for some patients, but for other people they become terminal conditions: • cancer • heart disease • hepatitis B • HIV/AIDS • meningitis	These diseases or conditions can sometimes be treated, but over time some patients reach a point at which treatment no longer gives much relief: • **Alzheimer's disease** • dementia • diabetes • muscular or spinal diseases such as **multiple sclerosis (MS)** and amyotrophic lateral sclerosis (ALS) • Parkinson's disease • stroke	Certain accidents that injure the brain, spinal cord, or vital organs can cause permanent damage, but not necessarily death: • automobile accidents • fire-related injuries • home accidents • shootings or other violent crimes • sports injuries • war injuries

Infant euthanasia

One of the most controversial topics in medicine involves the life of unborn children. The debate over **abortion** rights has raged for many years.

But another difficult question arises when a baby is born with severe, obvious health issues. In rare cases, babies are born with organs that are not fully formed, or brain, heart, or skin **disorders**. This raises difficult questions about whether a life should be ended to avoid unnecessary suffering.

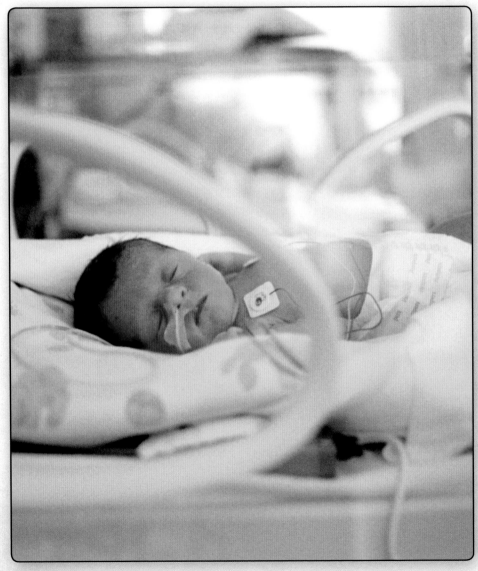

■ In rare cases, infant euthanasia is considered by doctors and parents. One difficulty is deciding the fate of a person who is alive but truly has no voice to speak for him or herself.

For instance, a baby in the Netherlands was born with Hallopeau–Siemens syndrome. This is a skin disorder in which the baby's skin comes off the body if touched by anyone. Doctors said the baby could have lived for 10 years with treatment, and they attempted to keep her alive – but she died of pneumonia after six months. In tragic cases like this, some doctors and even parents think it is best to allow the baby's life to end immediately rather than cause a child to endure more suffering.

Elder care

It is not always a particular disease that leads people to consider assisted suicide. Sometimes it is simply old age. Depending on where you live, life expectancy (the age to which most people will live) today is more than 75 years old. This is an average, so many people are living well into their eighties, nineties, and beyond. Compare this to about a century ago, in 1900, when the average life expectancy was just 47.

While many elderly people are able to stay active and alert, old age is a much sadder story for others. Some people whose spouses die years before them no longer have a companion to help them and keep them company in old age. They may have no other family to care for them and face years of ageing alone and helpless. Some elderly people also cannot afford the high cost of health care or assisted-living facilities. They struggle to buy their own food or do simple household chores on their own.

As a result, people who have already lived very long lives decide that they do not wish to suffer through any more years. They may choose to seek assistance in ending their lives.

DIFFICULT QUESTIONS

Most news stories about assisted suicide concern people with terminal diseases or brain and spinal cord injuries. But old age can leave a person just as desperate for a peaceful end to life. Do you think an elderly person choosing assisted suicide is the same as a person with terminal cancer? How are they similar or different?

Mental illness

For some people, mental illness makes life unbearable. In 2006 the government of Switzerland passed a law allowing assisted suicides for people with mental illnesses. These are illnesses that would not eventually lead to the person's death. The Swiss government said that people suffering from "incurable, permanent, severe psychological disorders" had the right to end their lives.

This decision added a new layer to the debate about assisted suicide. A person with a severe mental disorder does not have a physical condition that will cause his or her death. Rather, the patient's quality of life is at issue. But opponents of the laws also argue that people with severe mental illness are not capable of knowing what is best for themselves and should not be allowed to make these decisions.

■ Many people with mental illnesses are able to function and make decisions about their lives. Others, who have severe mental illnesses, cannot make clear decisions. Governments struggle with the rights of these people to choose suicide.

CASE STUDY

Reverend George Exoo

Reverend George D. Exoo is a Unitarian minister from Pennsylvania, USA. He has also helped more than 100 people end their lives. Reverend Exoo started with assisted suicide in the late 1990s, when a member of his church asked for help for a relative suffering from ALS, a disease of the brain and spinal cord also known as Lou Gehrig's disease. In the years since, Reverend Exoo has responded to requests from people with different medical conditions, including mental illness.

Because he has helped people without terminal illnesses, Reverend Exoo has become a controversial figure. Sometimes he travels to patients, sits by their bedsides, and helps them with their suicides. Other times, he may "coach" people over the phone to help them carry out the act on their own.

In 2002 he travelled to Dublin, Ireland, and assisted in the suicide of a woman with depression. After he returned to the United States, the Dublin police tracked down Reverend Exoo and attempted to receive permission from the US government to arrest him. Eventually, Exoo was arrested and placed in prison in 2007. But his case never went to trial. US law did not agree with Ireland's law, and the case was thrown out. Reverend Exoo was released from prison and allowed to continue doing his work.

DIFFICULT QUESTIONS

If your family has owned a pet for a long time, you may have had the sad experience of watching your beloved pet grow old and die. Dogs, cats, and other household pets can develop painful diseases that will eventually kill them. Most often, veterinarians recommend that the animal be "put to sleep" (euthanized), so that it does not have to suffer. If people can agree that this is a compassionate and acceptable procedure for pets, should the same logic apply to humans who are suffering? What do you think?

THE LONG DEATH OF TERRI SCHIAVO

Terri Schiavo lived a short life, but she suffered a long death. Her story highlights all the complexities of choosing to end the life of a patient.

Terri was a healthy 26-year-old woman when she suddenly collapsed in her home on February 25, 1990. Her husband, Michael, called the emergency services, but Terri's life had changed permanently before help could arrive. Due to lack of oxygen after her collapse, Terri suffered brain damage so severe that she would never reawaken or be herself again.

Searching for solutions

Terri was taken to a hospital and treated in intensive care, with Michael and her family at her side. Doctors advised that Terri would either die or come back to consciousness very quickly – but one day after another passed without any change. She was in a **coma**, unconscious and unable to breathe on her own. Days turned to weeks, and finally on 9 May, Terri was taken from the hospital, still in a coma. She was transferred to a long-term health care facility, where her doctors and family hoped she would recover.

Michael Schiavo and Terri's parents, Bob and Mary Schindler, attempted one treatment after another. They sought the advice of many different doctors in different states. They spent hundreds of thousands of dollars on Terri's care. But no solutions could be found. No doctors could even identify the cause of Terri's original collapse in 1990.

Family struggles

By 1993 Michael and Terri's parents were arguing over the best course of care for Terri. Because he was her husband, Michael had been appointed Terri's **legal guardian** by the court back in 1990. Three years later, the Schindlers wanted to take over their daughter's care, but a judge refused their request.

Terri passed from a coma into a **vegetative state** (see box below). Michael Schiavo believed the doctors who told him there was no hope for Terri to recover. Based on memories of past conversations with his wife, Michael thought that if Terri could communicate, she would say that she would not want to continue in this state – that she would not want to continue putting her family through their suffering.

So, in 1998, Michael went to court to ask permission to have doctors remove Terri's **feeding tube**, an act that would eventually end her life by depriving her of nourishment. Michael later said, "I was doing something that Terri wanted. And I couldn't give up on her."

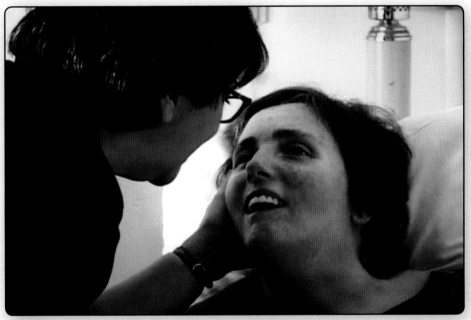

■ This excerpt from a video of Terri Schiavo during her hospitalisation shows her in a very rare moment when she appears to respond to her mother.

WHAT IS A VEGETATIVE STATE?

A vegetative state is a condition that is caused by brain damage and that leaves a person with little ability to move and very little, if any, ability to communicate. Unlike being in a coma, a person in a vegetative state may be awake much of the time. It is sometimes called a "wakeful unconsciousness".

Legal battles

The Schindlers believed Michael was giving up on Terri. They believed that their daughter would want to fight to live. Removing the feeding tube, they believed, was the equivalent of murdering their daughter. They fought their son-in-law in court, and more than a year and a half later, a judge issued a ruling. On 11 February 2000, Judge George Greer said that Terri would have wanted to have her feeding tube removed, and he ordered doctors to do so.

A HOT TOPIC

Terri's case and the court battles surrounding her became a worldwide news story. Religious leaders, legal scholars, politicians, and ordinary citizens chose sides. They argued on the Internet, on television news programmes, and in the streets. Daily protests were staged in which people supported either Michael's right to end Terri's life, or Terri's parents' right to keep their daughter alive.

■ Protesters who supported Terri's right to live.

The issue exposed a society divided on the issue of euthanasia and assisted suicide. Some people argued on religious grounds, saying it was God's decision when a person should die, not a spouse's and not a court's (see pages 34 to 37). Others argued for individual rights, saying that a person should have the right to control his or her own death – or that of a husband or wife.

But the Schindlers **appealed** the judge's ruling, and the appeals continued for years – all the way to the US Supreme Court, the highest legal authority in the United States. Twice Terri's feeding tube was removed based on court rulings. But both times the tube was removed, it had to then be reinserted due to new legal challenges from the Schindlers.

The case became a sensation in major media throughout the United States. Meanwhile, Terri continued to live in a vegetative state, unresponsive and barely alive.

Final resolution

Finally, on 25 February 2005, Judge Greer again ordered that the tube be removed, and doctors did so on 18 March – for the last time.

In the coming days, the US Congress approved a bill that would send the Schiavo case to a federal court for review, and US President George W. Bush signed the bill into law on 21 March. But despite these efforts, a judge in Florida refused to order the feeding tube to be reinserted. On 31 March 2005, Terri Schiavo finally died.

During Terri's 15-year struggle, people around the world came to grips with one of the most difficult issues to comprehend: Does anyone have the right to bring a human life to an end?

MEDICAL QUESTIONS

Fuelling the debate about Terri Schiavo's right to die were disagreements over the true nature of Terri's condition. Some doctors said that Terri was in a life-long vegetative state, with no hope of ever recovering. Other doctors said it was possible she could recover.

In 2002, Terri's parents released video clips of Terri in **hospice** care. The very brief snippets showed that Terri was somewhat alert, sometimes smiling and responding to conversation, although she was unable to speak. This lack of clear medical answers made the debate that much more intense.

THE ACTS OF EUTHANASIA AND ASSISTED SUICIDE

Clearly, the decision to end a patient's life is an incredibly complex and difficult one. The issue of how the life is medically brought to an end is also complex and controversial. When a person who is suffering from a severe illness or that person's family chooses to end the patient's life, their two options are usually euthanasia and assisted suicide.

Euthanasia

Euthanasia is when a **physician** intentionally ends a patient's life because the patient or the patient's family instructs the doctor to do so. Doctors can do this in several different ways, each intended to cause no pain, or as little pain as possible.

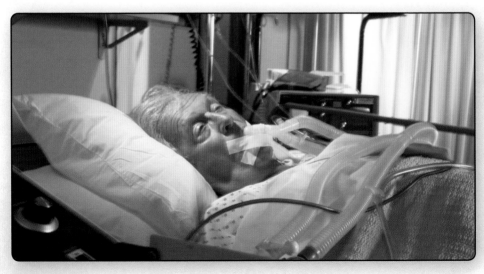

■ A **ventilator** is a machine that forces air into and out of the lungs when a patient's brain cannot control this function

Passive euthanasia

Passive euthanasia involves letting someone die by stopping (or not starting) medical treatments that could keep a person alive. For instance, a person may need a ventilator machine in order to breathe. If a doctor does not start the ventilator, this is passive euthanasia – the patient will die because the treatment was not given.

Active euthanasia

Active euthanasia involves causing someone to die by committing a specific act that ends a patient's life. For instance, if a doctor injects a large dose of pain medication that stops the patient's heart or other organs, the patient will die directly because of this action.

ACTIVE OR PASSIVE EUTHANASIA?

The difference between active and passive euthanasia is sometimes blurry. People hold different opinions on the matter. For instance, when Terri Schiavo was allowed to starve without a feeding tube, some people thought this was passive euthanasia, because nobody provided medical treatment to keep Terri alive. Others thought that removing her feeding tube was an action on the part of her doctor, and that Terri therefore died from active euthanasia. And others went further, calling the act murder – the intentional killing of another human being. What do you think?

Assisted suicide

A physician causes euthanasia, however a physician, a relative, a friend, or the patient him or herself may be involved in assisted suicide.

When physicians play a part in assisted suicide, it is called **physician-assisted suicide**. In such cases a doctor or other medical professional provides advice, medical supplies, or equipment. The physician might be present, but no physical assistance is given. For instance, a doctor may instruct a patient exactly how to take a dose of medicine that will cause death. It is then up to the patient to take this medicine without the doctor's help.

How it's done

When the difficult decision has been made to pursue euthanasia or assisted suicide, another set of equally troubling decisions must be made: how to do it. Speed and painlessness are the two key factors in determining the best way to end a patient's life.

Performing active euthanasia

In cases of active euthanasia, the most common method involves injecting chemicals into the patient's bloodstream. A doctor will inject a sleep-inducing drug into the patient so he or she is fully unconscious and can feel no pain. Then, the doctor will inject other chemicals that will cause immediate death by making the heart stop.

Doctors performed active euthanasia more commonly in the past. Today, if active euthanasia is ever performed, it is done in secret. A doctor performing this act would probably be open to charges of murder. So when active euthanasia occurs, it is rarely reported publicly.

Performing passive euthanasia

In order to commit passive euthanasia, a physician might follow one of these methods:

- remove a feeding tube
- remove a breathing apparatus or other life-support system
- stop medications or not perform life-saving surgery
- not perform **cardiopulmonary resuscitation (CPR)**, the emergency process forcing blood and oxygen to circulate when a patient has stopped breathing, or his or her heart has stopped beating

Performing assisted suicide

When a doctor assists in a suicide, he or she is only providing advice and possibly materials that a person needs. Assisted suicides might take place in a hospital, a hospice, or a nursing home. Or it could occur in the patient's home.

In most cases, a physician will give a patient a prescription for a drug such as sleeping pills, as well as instructions on how much of the drug to take. Or a physician may explain to a patient how to inhale carbon monoxide gas. There are other methods as well, but whatever the method, assisted suicide is perhaps one of the most difficult acts any person is faced with in a lifetime. If the patient is planning to perform the act, he or she usually needs a companion to make sure it is done properly. Mistakes in such cases can allow the person to survive, but with additional medical issues.

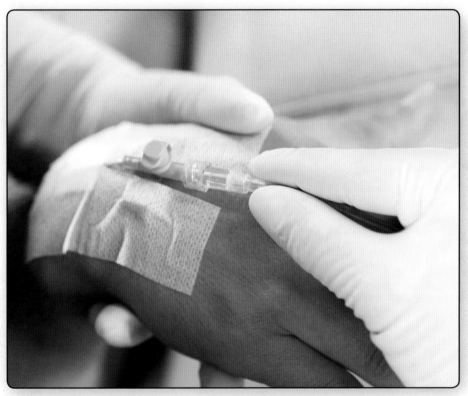

■ Active euthanasia commonly involved injecting chemicals into a patient's bloodstream. But because of the risk involved to doctors, active euthanasia is rarely performed today.

DIFFICULT QUESTIONS

The job of a doctor or nurse is to help people recover from illnesses. But sometimes physicians are asked to end a life instead. If you were a doctor or nurse, do you think you could assist someone in a suicide?

JACK KEVORKIAN

Dr Jack Kevorkian is perhaps the most famous person who has performed assisted suicides.

In the spring of 1990, a woman named Janet Adkins was in the early stages of Alzheimer's disease, an incurable disease. The condition promised a gradual **deterioration** of her mental capacity and years of medical treatment. Janet wanted an early exit. So, she arranged for Kevorkian to help her end her life.

Kevorkian was a US doctor who had been advertising that he could counsel people on death. It turned out he offered more than counselling. On 4 June 1990, Janet climbed into Kevorkian's 1968 Volkswagen van. In the back of the van was a small bed and a simple-looking homemade machine with several bottles of chemicals hanging upside down. Kevorkian would come to call it the "Thanatron", which in Greek means "instrument of death". Most people would call it his "suicide machine".

Janet lay down on the bed, and Kevorkian inserted an IV (intravenous) needle into a vein in her arm. At this point, the IV sent harmless saline solution into her body. Then, the doctor showed her a button to press. Janet pressed it, and a poisonous substance, potassium chloride, flowed into her veins. Kevorkian recalls that Janet whispered, "thank you", before she died moments later. Janet Adkins was the first person Kevorkian helped to die.

Arrest and release

After Kevorkian called the police to report Janet's death, he was arrested and charged with murder. The charges were eventually dismissed because the judge did not consider Kevorkian's act to be murder, and Michigan did not have a law banning assisted suicide.

The arrest did not stop Kevorkian. In 1991 he assisted in the suicides of two more women in Michigan, resulting in another arrest and another trial. Again, Kevorkian was set free. This cycle continued through the 1990s. The Michigan authorities continued to try to stop Kevorkian, but legal technicalities continually got in their way. The Michigan government twice passed laws banning assisted suicide, but the state supreme court overruled the laws both times.

■ Dr Jack Kevorkian poses with his "suicide machine". The machine was designed so that he would only need to connect an IV line from the machine to the patient while the machine fed harmless fluids into the patient's body. Then the patient would press a button that would switch the flow to a deadly drug or chemical.

Fame

With each arrest and trial, Kevorkian's fame grew around the world. A poll taken in 1993 showed that 94 per cent of Americans had heard of him, and at one point 58 per cent approved of him. Perhaps the fact that he was a kind-looking, white-haired man in his sixties helped his image in the public eye. Maybe it was his blunt honesty. Maybe people admired his willingness to stand up for his beliefs. Several times when Kevorkian was being held in jail, he went on hunger strikes in protest. These dramatic acts earned him even more headlines.

Kevorkian became a strange kind of celebrity. People started using the slang term "Kevork" for "suicide". Kevorkian was referred to as "Dr Death". It was actually a nickname he had had since the 1950s, when he did research into the nature of death by photographing the eyes of dying patients.

■ In 2010, the actor Al Pacino portrayed Kevorkian in a television film called *You Don't Know Jack*.

The last suicide

In 1998 Kevorkian helped a man called Thomas Youk, a patient with ALS, commit suicide. As part of a news story on Kevorkian, the television programme *60 Minutes* broadcast video of the suicide itself, which created a firestorm of discussion and controversy among doctors, lawyers, and the public. This time, Kevorkian was arrested again, put on trial, and found guilty. He was sentenced to 10 to 25 years in prison.

After serving eight years of his sentence, Kevorkian was set free in June 2007. In an interview with *CNN* in 2010, Kevorkian said, "I didn't do it to end a life, I did it to end the suffering the patient's going through. The patient [was] obviously suffering. What's a doctor supposed to do – turn his back?" Under the conditions of his release, he is not allowed to assist in any suicides.

■ Kevorkian was tried in court many times during the 1990s.

ADVANCE DECISIONS

The patients who were helped by Jack Kevorkian made their wishes known. But not all patients have this opportunity.

For instance, if a woman in her thirties is injured in a fire and is rushed into an emergency room unconscious and close to death, how can doctors know what kind of care the person wants? The person might be perfectly healthy and want every measure taken to keep her alive. Or the person could have terminal cancer and only have weeks to live – she may not want to survive.

The purpose of doctors, nurses, and hospitals is to cure any ailment, no matter what it takes. But some people may not want to be cured, and these patients cannot always speak up.

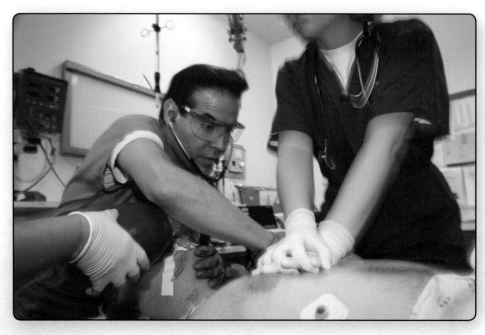

■ In the rush of action in an emergency room, medical staff are primarily focused on saving lives in any way they can.

Advance decisions

In recent years people have started writing **living wills** or **advance decisions**, which are documents containing their wishes about their medical care. An advance decision is used to state when a person wishes to refuse medical treatment. People write these directions down when they are healthy and calm and can think clearly. They put the documents in a place where close relatives know to find them. In the event of an emergency, the documents can be used to tell physicians how to treat the person.

Lasting Power of Attorney

If a child is ill and doctors need to ask permission about medical procedures, they know to ask the child's parents. But if an adult is ill and cannot communicate, it may not be clear who should be making decisions. The patient's spouse? What if the patient is unmarried or divorced? Or what if the patient's adult children object to the spouse's decisions? These sorts of disagreements came to the forefront during the Terri Schiavo case.

To avoid such problems, people are making a Lasting Power of Attorney Health and Welfare (LPA HW) order. This is a legal document that states which adult will make all decisions for a person if that person cannot communicate or make decisions for other reasons. These decisions can include specific ones about medical treatment or more general decisions about where that person will live.

DIFFICULT QUESTIONS

A best friend or a close relative is usually the person who is given Lasting Power of Attorney. With that job comes tremendous responsibility, including possibly making the decision to end the life of a friend or loved one. Do you think you could make decisions if you were given Lasting Power of Attorney?

DNR

The best-known advance decision is a **Do Not Resuscitate (DNR) order**. In a medical emergency, a person may suffer cardiac and/or respiratory arrest, causing the heart and breathing to stop working. Emergency medical technicians are trained to perform CPR when this happens – this can get the heart and lungs working again. Drugs and an electronic shock (defibrillation) might also be used.

Sometimes CPR will indeed save a patient, who could then return to normal health. But sometimes CPR is not effective and the patient dies. In still other cases, CPR may get the heart beating again, yet leave the person in otherwise poor health. For instance, if the brain is deprived of blood for too long, the person may be left in a coma, although alive. Also the actions of pressing on the chest to perform CPR can be damageing. CPR can cause a collapsed lung. Or for elderly patients with weak bones, CPR can even break ribs and lead to serious, painful complications.

So, to avoid the trauma and risks of **resuscitation**, some people simply choose not to allow it. They use a DNR order to instruct physicians to not resuscitate them if their heart stops beating or if they stop breathing.

PROBLEMS WITH DNR ORDERS

Sometimes people write their DNR orders on their own. These orders can be written with mistakes or can be vague. For instance, many people write in a DNR order that they do not want "extreme measures" taken to save their lives. But they do not define what they mean by "extreme measures". Does this mean patients do not want CPR performed? Does it mean they do not want to be placed on a ventilator? Does this mean they do not want to be fed fluids to be kept alive if they fall into a coma? Because DNR orders can be confusing or incomplete, many doctors argue that DNR orders do not always serve the best interests of patients.

Refusal of food and fluids

The Voluntary Refusal of Food and Fluids (VRFF) or a Patient Refusal of Nutrition and Hydration (PRNH) are other kinds of advance decisions. Both are ways for people to state in writing that if their health condition reaches a certain point, they do not want doctors to give them food or water, thus allowing them to starve to death. With this statement in writing, a person can remove any doubt about how a physician should act as the patient nears death.

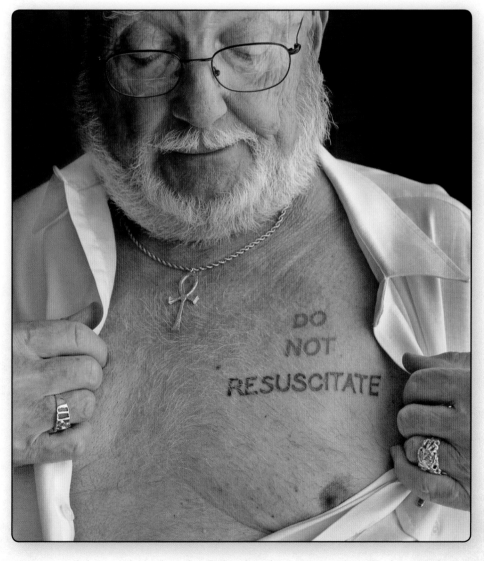

■ Some people leave no doubt about their DNR wishes. This man tattooed a DNR order on his chest so that no doctor or emergency medical crew can overlook it.

Problems with advance decisions

While it seems logical that advanced planning is a good idea, advance decisions can sometimes create problems rather than solve them. Many advance decisions are not written properly. As we have seen on page 28, DNR orders are often open to interpretation and can cause confusion for doctors.

Dr Susan Hickman of the Indiana University School of Nursing in the United States did a study of advance decisions, and she found many flaws. For instance, she says that people often write that they do not want life-saving treatment if they are "close to death". But they do not define what they mean by "close to death". One doctor could interpret that as one hour away from dying. Another doctor could think that means a week away from dying.

■ Many people with disabilities or injuries live normal, fulfilling lives. Some doctors argue that, because modern medicine can do so much for patients, people should not be quick to assume that they need to have a DNR order to keep from experiencing terrible suffering.

Do doctors know best?

Some opponents of euthanasia and assisted suicide further argue that when ordinary people try to give orders to doctors in advance, they are not allowing doctors to do their jobs. Doctors are trained to save lives and cure problems. They have the most complete knowledge about what is best to do in an emergency situation.

Dr Boris Veysman, Assistant Professor of Emergency Medicine at the Robert Wood Johnson Medical School in the United States, believes that many people do not understand the big picture when they write advance decisions. He wrote:

"Folks who say, 'When I get that sick, unplug me, don't let me suffer,' usually watched a depressing movie or saw someone dying miserably on life support. They've never been exposed to the other point of view or learned how the end of life can be done better. And they should hear it from a medical professional before making up their minds about something this important. In my role as a doctor, I've met countless disabled, disfigured, machine-supported people who enjoy living and wish to continue doing so as long as possible."

Dr Veysman goes on to say that he does not want a DNR order for himself. He wants as much treatment as possible to extend his life as long as possible.

Clearly, no single choice about when to end a life is right for every person and every situation. Even knowing a patient's wishes ahead of time does not always offer a clear course of action, as situations can often bring about unexpected realities.

TALKING THROUGH A TREATMENT PLAN

In non-emergency settings, many doctors are able to take the time to talk to all family members and make sure everyone agrees on a treatment plan. Dr Naren Kapadia, a US oncologist (a doctor who treats cancer patients) says that advance decisions "don't really mean anything until the person can't make a decision for himself. I have meetings with every member of the family until they all come to the same conclusion. I spend enough time to be sure I know what they want."

VIEWS ABOUT EUTHANASIA AND ASSISTED SUICIDE

The struggle over euthanasia and assisted suicide is complex. Many big ideas come into conflict when people try to decide what is right and wrong.

Ancient beliefs

The issues of euthanasia and assisted suicide are not new. Historians believe that in ancient Greece and Rome, babies born with serious deformities were euthanized. It is believed that physicians also helped people to die rather than force them to endure painful illness.

With the rise of Christianity, attitudes about suicide turned negative. Saint Thomas Aquinas (1225–1274) wrote: "It is altogether unlawful to kill oneself … Suicide is always a mortal sin, as being contrary to the natural law and to charity." Led by the teachings of the church, English common law banned suicide or punished those who assisted in it.

THE HIPPOCRATIC OATH

The attitudes of many ancient Greeks and Romans towards euthanasia and assisted suicide seemed to go against the famous Hippocratic Oath, created by the physician Hippocrates. This oath said: "To please no one will I prescribe a deadly drug nor give advice which may cause his death." In other words, physicians must never contribute to a patient's death. Clearly, there have always been differing viewpoints about the issues of euthanasia and assisted suicide.

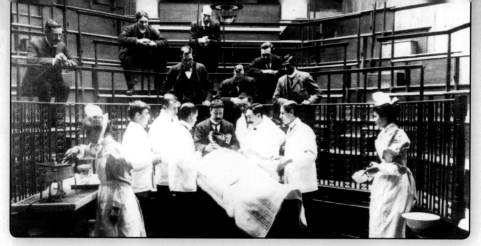
■ In the 1890s, doctors were still beginning to understand how to use painkilling medication.

Later, in the 1700s and 1800s, medical science began to quickly understand the workings of the human body. Treatment of disease advanced, and scientists began using the drugs morphine and ether to help patients deal with pain. Doctors also used these and other drugs to cause patients' deaths to relieve their suffering.

The 19th and 20th centuries

In the 1800s and 1900s, most nations passed laws banning euthanasia and assisted suicide. One reason was the belief that it is dangerous to allow some kinds of assisted suicide, because it could lead to greater abuses.

In the 1940s in Nazi Germany, this nightmare played out in reality. In addition to murdering millions of Jewish people and other minorities, the Nazis attempted to eliminate mentally and physically disabled people throughout Germany. German doctors and nurses were forced to evaluate some children and disabled people, and those who failed their evaluations were sent to special clinics. There, they were killed by injection of drugs or by starvation. Historians believe the Nazis killed more than 200,000 people in this way.

MODERN-DAY DANGERS?

To this day, some people fear that disabled people could be threatened if doctors are allowed more freedom to euthanize patients. They believe this opens the door for a government to decide that certain "undesirable" groups in society should be eliminated . . . just as the Nazis did. What do you think?

Religion and suicide

As seen with the example of Thomas Aquinas, religion has played a part in people's opinions about euthanasia and assisted suicide for many centuries. Today, as medicine introduces new technologies at a rapid pace, religious belief is especially relevant in considering this difficult issue.

Sanctity of life

One of the core beliefs of many religions, including Christianity, is the **sanctity of life**. The word "sanctity" means "holy" or "sacred". There are many ways of interpreting the ideas of "holy" and "sacred", but two key ideas are:

- Something that is holy or sacred is "godly". It is a part of our lives that is connected to God.
- Something that is holy or sacred is untouchable. It is something that should not be violated or altered by humans.

So, to say that people believe in the sanctity of life is to say that human life is connected to God and must not be violated. This makes it wrong to end a human life intentionally. In the view of many religions, to murder someone clearly violates the sanctity of life, and so does committing suicide.

CHRISTIANITY AND THE SANCTITY OF LIFE

Even in cases of suffering or a terminal disease, many Christians still uphold the sanctity of life. They believe that even a life with such suffering is sacred and must not be violated, and every life must be allowed to end on its own. It is up to God to call an end to each life on Earth, not up to doctors, governments, or even the individual person.

Within the Christian religion, there are disagreements on this point, however. Many Christians also accept that there are circumstances when euthanasia or assisted suicide might be an acceptable path to choose.

Sanctity versus quality of life

Religious leaders often point out that the sanctity of life is more important than the quality of life. They argue that God loves all people equally – whether they are rich or poor, beautiful or ugly, young or old, tall or short. Along the same lines, it is taught that God loves all humans equally, even if they have physical or mental disabilities, or if they are terminally ill. Good health, intelligence, physical beauty, athletic ability … all of these factors are qualities of life. They should not have anything to do with whether a person deserves to live or die.

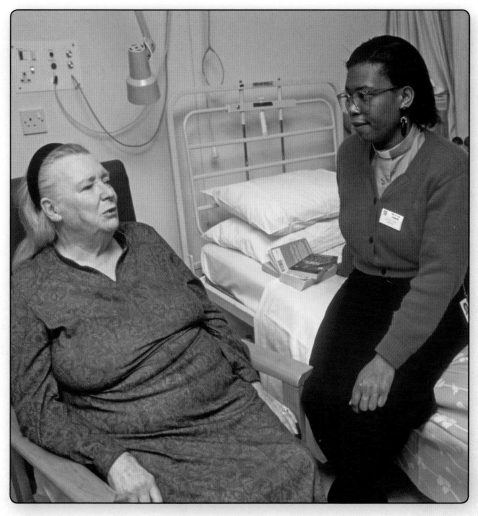

■ Religious clergy spend countless hours counselling patients through long and painful illnesses. Many Christians support the idea that although suffering is difficult to endure, it does not justify suicide.

Religious viewpoints

Today's religions have differing attitudes about euthanasia and assisted suicide. Even within religious groups, it is sometimes difficult to pin down one consistent set of beliefs. Sometimes the religion itself offers differing views, and sometimes individuals who follow a religion disagree with its teachings. The table below provides a summary of the views of six major world religions on the debate over euthanasia and assisted suicide.

Major religions' views on euthanasia and assisted suicide

Religion	Views
Christianity	There are several different types of Christianity, called denominations (Catholic, Anglican, Lutheran, Greek Orthodox, Presbyterian, Protestant, and more), yet all share a common belief: the sanctity of life makes suicide and euthanasia sins that should not be allowed. Here are a few examples of how different Christian denominations stand on the issue: • The Roman Catholic Church is firmly opposed to all forms of euthanasia and assisted suicide. • The Church of England opposes any change in the law or medical practice to make assisted suicide permissible. • The Evangelical Lutheran Church in the United States declares that some forms of passive euthanasia are acceptable, but the church remains opposed to other forms of assisted suicide and euthanasia. • Protestantism also allows for passive euthanasia.
Judaism	Orthodox (the most traditional) Judaism treats suicide and euthanasia as a sin. However, Jewish law does allow for some means of passive euthanasia. Today, there are more liberal sects, or groups, in Judaism (Conservative, Reform, and more) in which religious law is followed to different degrees. Many Jews today believe it is acceptable to follow their own personal sense of **ethics** on issues such as assisted suicide rather than follow strict Jewish law.

Religion	Views
Islam	Islam does not allow any form of suicide, including euthanasia and assisted suicide. Muslims (followers of the Islamic faith) are allowed, however, to refuse medical treatment.
Hinduism	Hindu philosophy offers the idea that helping a person end a painful life is a good deed, yet this does not really allow for euthanasia or assisted suicide. Both practices are considered to be sins.
Buddhism	A key idea in Buddhism is the individual's progression from one life to the next; death is seen as a transition, not an end. Buddhism does not offer a single, strict rule on whether euthanasia or assisted suicide are right or wrong.
Shinto	Most followers of the Shinto faith (the largest religion in Japan) believe that passive euthanasia is acceptable.

ASSISTED SUICIDE LAWS AROUND THE WORLD

In recent years, science, religion, and law have continually collided over many issues. Science and medicine continue to lead humans in new directions. Sometimes these new directions conflict with religious beliefs. Governments frequently step in when they believe individual rights are in danger, or if the common good of society is at risk. The case of euthanasia and assisted suicide is a perfect example of this cycle.

Australia's Rights of the Terminally Ill Act

On 1 July 1996, an historic occurrence took place in Australia. A doctor helped a terminally ill man commit suicide – the first time in the 20th century that a legal physician-assisted suicide took place.

RIGHTS OF THE TERMINALLY ILL ACT

Australia's Rights of the Terminally Ill Act was a law that allowed people to commit suicide and be assisted by a physician. The key rules according to the law were:

1. The person had to be 18 years of age or older, and had to be able to make decisions. The person could not be suffering from a mental disorder that would get in the way of making such a decision.
2. The person had to get three doctors to agree with the decision.
3. The person would have to wait nine days after submitting the application before the actual suicide could take place.

The previous year, the government of Australia's Northern Territory had passed the Rights of the Terminally Ill Act. The Australian Medical Association, religious leaders, and government officials were outraged by the passage of this law, yet it became official in the spring of 1995.

A little over a year later, a patient dying of cancer was the first person to carry out the rights allowed in the law. The man wrote before he died: "The church and the law should be separate. If you disagree with voluntary euthanasia, don't use it, but please don't deny me the right to use it if I want to." His doctor used a computerized machine that delivered a **lethal** dose of drugs.

Less than a year later, however, the law was overturned. Four people were legally euthanized before the Australian government passed a new law in March 1997 that outlawed assisted suicide. All forms of assisted suicide have remained illegal ever since.

■ In the Northern Territory of Australia, a groundbreaking challenge to assisted suicide laws broke out following a legal physician-assisted suicide in 1996.

Australia's stand on assisted suicide

Since the Rights of the Terminally Ill Act was overturned, Australia has gone on to become one of the strictest anti-assisted suicide countries in the world. In May 2009 the government banned the distribution of an online book cowritten by Dr Philip Nitschke (see below), the doctor who performed the first legal assisted suicide in 1996. The book provides detailed instructions on peaceful ways for people to commit suicide.

CASE STUDY

Dr Philip Nitschke

After Dr Jack Kevorkian hit the headlines in the 1990s as the "lone ranger" of assisted suicide, other doctors around the world also took up the cause. Like Kevorkian, Dr Philip Nitschke of Australia opposed the laws that he believed were wrong, but he also took his cause to greater lengths.

Nitschke assisted in the suicides of all four people who took advantage of Australia's brief period when assisted suicide was legal, from 1996 to 1997. Since assisted suicide has become illegal, however, Nitschke has limited himself to giving advice and not actually assisting with suicides. He tells people which drugs are best-suited to provide a peaceful death and advises them on how to travel to other countries to obtain these drugs. He tells people how they can hack into websites to find information or to order drugs if those websites are blocked in Australia. But he doesn't do anything illegal himself.

Nitschke has become an **activist**, a person who makes it his purpose to inform the public about an issue and who tries to create changes in laws and in society. He speaks in public, appears on television, and writes books to promote the cause. He believes that individuals should have the right to control their own lives. He says, "What [bothers] me most about people who oppose this issue is that they are quite keen [eager] to shove their worldview down other people's throats."

■ Dr Philip Nitschke, an Australian activist who supports assisted suicide and euthanasia rights.

Oregon's Death with Dignity Act

While assisted suicide was debated in Australia, the world took notice.

In the United States, the individual states are able to pass laws on issues like this – as long as the laws do not conflict with the federal laws that cover citizens of the entire nation. In 1997 the state of Oregon became the first US state to pass a law allowing assisted suicide. Called the Death with Dignity Act, the law was passed in October 1997 and went into effect in 1998. The following year, Washington state passed a similar law.

The Oregon law is written to limit the right to assisted suicide to a very small set of circumstances:

- No children can be euthanised – the person has to be aged 18 or older.
- Patients have to be residents of Oregon.
- Patients have to be healthy enough to communicate clearly and make sound decisions about their own health care.
- Patients have to have a terminal illness that a doctor says gives them six months or less to live.

■ US state laws such as Oregon's Death with Dignity Act have caused people to protest vigorously on both sides of the issue.

Complications

In the first nine years after the law went into effect, there were 292 officially reported assisted suicides in Oregon. There were also many reports of complications and difficulties. For instance, sometimes people did not, or could not, carry out taking the lethal drugs successfully. Others needed help from a spouse or friend, who did not know how to handle the situation. In some cases, patients survived – with further medical complications. Also, not all doctors understood the exact rules about patients being residents of the state of Oregon.

Opponents say this proves that there is no way to guarantee that these laws can be carried out perfectly.

CASE STUDY

Robert Baxter

Robert Baxter was a tough man. He fought in the Korean War for the US Marines. After his military service, he became a lorry driver and drove long-haul routes for nearly 50 years.

In 2009 Robert had been struggling with leukaemia, a kind of cancer, for 12 years. His doctors told him it was terminal. The only way he could fight off the disease was by having **chemotherapy** treatments, which caused nausea and other reactions that he simply could not stand anymore. He decided he wanted a doctor to help him die. When no doctor would agree to help him, he decided to go to court in his home state of Montana.

Robert was not just trying to get assisted suicide to be allowed by law. Instead, his lawyers challenged the constitution of the state. They argued that when a doctor would not help him die, Robert's constitutional rights were violated. They argued that assisted suicide was the same as the right to free speech or the right to vote – in other words, a right protected under a constitution.

Robert Baxter won his case. But on the very day that the judge announced the ruling, Robert died of leukaemia.

Switzerland and Dignitas

Outside of the United States, the only countries where some forms of assisted suicide are legal are in Europe.

Switzerland has the longest history of allowing assisted suicide. To be precise, there is no Swiss law saying that assisted suicide is legal. However, a 1942 law says that suicide is only illegal if it is done for "selfish" reasons. This has opened the door to the interpretation that the suicide of a person who wishes to escape the pain of illness is not acting selfishly, and is therefore legal.

This has led to Switzerland becoming a kind of magnet for people seeking assistance with suicide. The Swiss organization Dignitas was founded in 1998 and assists foreign patients in carrying out their suicides. People travel from European countries and around the world so that Dignitas can handle their cases in Switzerland (see Case Study on the right). More than half of the people Dignitas has helped have come from Germany.

Assisted suicide in the Netherlands and Belgium

The Netherlands also has liberal laws relating to assisted suicide. In 2002 the Dutch government legalized physician-assisted suicide, making it the first nation in the world to come out and say that this practice is entirely legal. Patients must be examined by two doctors, must have a terminal illness, and must pass through several other regulations before the procedure is approved. About a month after the Dutch law was passed in 2002, Belgium passed a similar law.

A DIFFICULT QUESTION

Would you risk going to prison for helping a loved one to end his or her life, rather than watch that person suffer against their wishes?

CASE STUDY

Daniel James

Englishman Daniel James was a 23-year-old rugby player when he was paralyzed in an accident in 2007. In a training session, his spine was dislocated when other players landed on him.

Daniel's medical condition was not terminal. Doctors advised he might live a long time paralyzed from the chest down. Millions of people have lived productive, happy lives with such disabilities. Daniel, however, could not imagine such a life for himself. A life-long athlete, he decided he would rather die than live the rest of his years in a wheelchair.

Daniel asked his parents to help him, so they took him to Dignitas in Switzerland. His parents wrote, "His death was an extremely sad loss … but no doubt a welcome relief from the 'prison' he felt his body had become."

■ Many disabled athletes are able to use wheelchairs to participate in a wide variety of sports. But for others, making the transition to a life that doesn't include the full use of their body can be unthinkable.

Assisted suicide in the United Kingdom

In the United Kingdom, euthanasia and physician-assisted suicide are illegal. But several high-profile cases have forced the government and the public to examine their attitudes, beginning with the story of Tony Bland (see Case Study on the right).

The government has been challenged several times to allow more freedom for patients. In 2007 a law was proposed that would allow terminally ill patients to be prescribed drugs that they could use to commit suicide. The law was not passed.

In 2008 a public prosecutor, Keir Starmer, said that charges would not automatically be brought against people who assisted seriously ill or injured people in their suicides. This promise was tested in the case of Daniel James (see Case Study on page 45). Under British law, Daniel James' parents should have been charged with illegally assisting in a suicide. But Starmer's promise stood up, and the parents were not charged with a crime.

A major question remained: If relatives wanted to take loved ones abroad to places like Switzerland to die, would they be breaking the law, or would they be excused? The case of Debbie Purdy (see Case Study on page 48) made the government examine this issue very closely. As a result, in July 2009, the government said it would establish **tribunals** to examine each case individually and tell the people involved whether or not their intended actions would be within the law.

In 2010 Starmer revised the guidelines on assisted suicide. The new guidelines focus less on a person's medical condition and more on the reasons a person chooses suicide. The government lists 22 "public interest factors" that are considered in whether or not a person will be prosecuted for assisting in a suicide. They include:

- whether the victim had reached a clear, voluntary decision to commit suicide
- whether the suspect (the person who assists in the suicide) might benefit from the victim's death (for instance, by inheriting money)
- whether the suspect reports the victim's suicide to the police and co-operates with the investigation.

CASE STUDY

Tony Bland

On 15 April 1989, a football match turned from a sporting event into horror. The Hillsborough stadium in Sheffield was the scene of one of the worst sporting tragedies of all time. A total of 96 Liverpool fans lost their lives. As more and more fans rushed into the stadium through a narrow tunnel, a disaster resulted at the other end, where people were blocked by a fence.

Ninety-four people died that day – crushed to death, suffocated, or injured in other ways, and a 14-year-old boy died four days later. Nineteen-year-old Tony Bland survived the crush with brain damage and was taken to a hospital in a coma. Tony survived in a persistent vegetative state for nearly four more years.

Tony's parents fought for – and won – government permission for his doctors to turn off his life-support systems, allowing him to die in March 1993. This led to a 1993 law that basically allowed passive euthanasia. Under the law, "omissions" are allowed – that is, doctors are allowed to not apply, or omit, life-saving care.

■ The aftermath of the tragic Hillsborough stadium incident, which caused 96 deaths.

CASE STUDY

Debbie Purdy

Debbie Purdy was already experiencing symptoms of multiple sclerosis (MS) in 1995 when she fell in love with Omar Puente, a musician from Cuba. After they were married they lived in England, where Omar helped care for her, and her disease progressed. MS is a disease of the brain and spinal cord. It can affect people differently and can develop gradually over many years. It produces many symptoms, including muscle aches that lead to weakness in the arms and legs. It can affect speech, vision, hearing, and reasoning.

As the years passed, Debbie realized that she could not possibly stand the rest of her life with MS. She already lived in increasing pain, spent much of her time in a wheelchair, could not sleep well, and could not use a knife and fork. She knew she would eventually be unable to communicate or care for herself. She knew she needed to exit life.

Debbie decided that she would have to travel to Switzerland to seek the help of Dignitas (see page 44) in helping her die. She wanted to wait as long as possible for that day to come. But she would eventually be unable to travel alone, and her husband would have to travel to help her. What Debbie and Omar did not know was whether this would place Omar at risk of arrest.

Debbie fought a long, public battle with the British government, attempting to get the government to issue very clear guidelines about who would be prosecuted for assisting in suicides. As we have seen, the government eventually determined it would have experts examine each case individually. In the case of Debbie and Omar, the government said that Omar could help Debbie go to Switzerland when they decided the time was right. He would not be prosecuted.

This meant that Debbie and Omar could wait many more years before she would feel the need to end her life. She said, "I'm ecstatic. . . . I think people are beginning to realize now that this is not about a right to die; it is about a right to live." As of 2010, Debbie was still living out her life, enjoying her days with Omar, free to decide on the appropriate time to go to Switzerland.

■ Debbie Purdy is interviewed with her husband, Omar, at her side.

THE WAY FORWARD

Nothing is certain in life, except the fact that all living creatures will one day reach the end of their lives. But predicting when or how a person will die can be tricky. A patient can be told he or she has a terminal case of cancer with a brief amount of time to live. In many cases, that amount of time can extend by months or even years. In rare cases, seemingly miraculous recoveries do occur.

Defying the odds

In the same Hillsborough stadium disaster that eventually led to Tony Bland's assisted suicide (see page 47), another young man suffered very similar injuries. Twenty-two-year-old Andrew Devine suffered brain damage after being deprived of oxygen during the stadium crush. Like Tony, Andrew survived in a vegetative state. But eight years later, he started showing signs of consciousness and emerged from his vegetative state, much to the amazement of his doctors. Still severely disabled, he continues to try to improve and has gone on with his life.

A miraculous recovery

In 2009, 87-year-old Bob Sawyer of Massachusetts, USA, was seriously ill with lymphoma (a form of cancer). He developed pneumonia, and started losing weight rapidly when he could no longer swallow food. Doctors told his family to expect the worst, and preparations were made for his death.

A DIFFICULT QUESTION

Do you think euthanasia and assisted suicide should be banned because people can sometimes recover from serious illnesses, even if such recoveries are rare?

Yet somehow Bob turned a corner and recovered. Working with a nutritionist, he started gaining weight. Less than a year later, he won three gold medals in the Connecticut Senior Games in the 5K, 10K, and 20K bicycle races.

Waiting on scientific advances

In 2010 scientists began to think that a vegetative state is not necessarily as "brain dead" as once thought. Researchers found in brain scans that about 20 per cent of persistent-vegetative patients may actually be able to communicate in some manner.

Opponents of assisted suicide point to cases like this as evidence that people should not be allowed to intervene in the course of illness and death. Sometimes doctors are just plain wrong in predicting whether or not a person will recover from an injury or illness. Medical advances can also possibly result in cures or new treatments that can help patients if they live long enough. For various reasons, unexpected recoveries do occur.

Supporters of assisted suicide, however, argue that such recoveries are rare and unpredictable. Meanwhile, countless individuals suffer through costly and painful medical treatment. Family members struggle as they watch loved ones deteriorate.

Referees of the end of life

The age of science provides individuals with immense knowledge about their bodies. It provides physicians with tremendous power to control and alter the quality of life – and the end of life. As we struggle with these issues, we continue to call on governments to act as referees and provide fair laws on what is the best and proper way to act.

■ Andrew Devine emerged from a vegetative state to a state described as "minimal consciousness".

GLOSSARY

abortion medical procedure that deliberately ends a pregnancy

active euthanasia causing someone to die; the act of ending a life to end pain and suffering, in which a physician performs an action that leads directly to the patient's death

activist person who works to change laws or to change commonly held ideas in society

advance decisions instructions that people write prior to a major medical procedure giving specific instructions on the medical treatment they do not want to have

Alzheimer's disease disease of the brain that usually ends the patient's life

appeal to object or fight a legal decision

assisted suicide form of suicide in which another person helps someone commit suicide

cardiopulmonary resuscitation (CPR) emergency medical procedure in which a heart is restarted or breathing is forced to restart

chemotherapy treatment to fight cancer symptoms in which chemicals are delivered into the body that destroy cancer cells

coma state of being permanently unconscious

deterioration decline; breakdown

diagnose to decide what disease or medical condition a person has

dignity respect; worthy of honour

disorder disease or medical condition in which an aspect of a person's health is not right

Do Not Resuscitate (DNR) order document that people write out that instructs physicians not to use CPR or other means to attempt to save their lives if they are near death

ethics moral principles; right and wrong

euthanasia doctor ending a patient's life to relieve pain and suffering

feeding tube tube that is inserted in a patient through the nose or mouth that delivers nutrition to a patient who cannot feed himself or herself

hospice medical-care facility where terminally ill patients receive treatment, not to cure disease but to ease pain

legal guardian person who has been given the power to make all legal and medical decisions for another person

lethal deadly

living will document that people write giving instructions on how they want their end-of-life treatment to be handled

multiple sclerosis (MS) disease of the brain and spinal cord

paralysed condition in which all or parts of the body cannot move

passive euthanasia letting someone die; the act of ending a life to end pain and suffering, in which a physician does not begin treatment or removes life-support treatment

physician doctor; person who is licensed to practise medicine

physician-assisted suicide form of suicide in which a doctor or nurse provides advice, instructions, or materials to the person who commits suicide

resuscitation act of bringing a body back to life after certain functions have stopped

sanctity of life religious idea that human lives are connected to God and must not be violated

stroke interruption of blood flow to the brain, causing brain damage

suicide intentionally killing oneself

terminal describes a disease that has reached a stage at which a physician is certain it will kill the patient

tribunal group of people who judge claims or disputes

vegetative state condition similar to a coma in which a person has little ability to move and very little, if any, ability to communicate

ventilator medical machine that keeps the body breathing by forcing air into the lungs

FURTHER INFORMATION

Books

Ethical Debates: Euthanasia, Kaye Stearman (Wayland, 2011)

Just the Facts: Euthanasia, Linda Jackson (Raintree, 2005)

Physician-Assisted Suicide, Alan Marzilli (Chelsea House, 2004)

Websites

www.bbc.co.uk/ethics/euthanasia/
The BBC website explains euthanasia and presents the arguments for and against.

www.nhs.uk/conditions/Euthanasiaandassistedsuicide/Pages/Introduction.aspx
The NHS website gives an explanation of the different types of euthanasia and assisted suicide as well as the legal position in different countries.

www.guardian.co.uk/society/assisted-suicide
The Guardian newspaper's website contains links to several articles on all sides of the assisted suicide issue.

Topics for further research

Assisted suicide laws in the United Kingdom

Assisted suicide and euthanasia are illegal in the UK. Try to find out more about the issues and the prison sentences that may be given out to people who break the law.

Hippocrates

Find out more about Hippocrates, the ancient Greek doctor who invented many of the rules and ideas we still use today in governing how doctors should and should not work.

Hurricane Katrina

Learn more about Hurricane Katrina, which devastated New Orleans, USA, in August 2005. Among the many tragedies of this disaster was the fate of sick and elderly patients in hospitals. Some were stranded in buildings without electricity or proper medication. Several hospital workers were later accused of euthanising some of these patients rather than allowing them to suffer through a certain death.

Life expectancy

With new advances in medicine, people live longer lives today than they did just a century ago. But it's not just medical cures for diseases that are extending our lives. We live in a safer, easier world than any other humans have experienced. Use the Internet to discover the reasons for our longer life expectancy.

INDEX